COUNTRY · EXPLORERS

T0011778

A Visit to

SOUTH AFRICA

By Charis Mather

BEARPORT
PUBLISHING

Minneapolis, Minnesota

Credits

All images are courtesy of Shutterstock.com, unless otherwise specified. With thanks to Getty Images, Thinkstock Photo, and iStockphoto.

Cover – OlenaPalaguta, mitchFOTO. ModernNomad. 2–3 – SCStock. 4–5 – Nadezda Stoyanova, max dallocco. 6–7 – QQ7, Nok Lek. 8–9 – AlexAnton, V_E, Alkhutov Dmitry. 10–11 – DS_93, Liliya Kulianionak. 12–13 – lovelypeace, stefano carniccio. 14–15 – TTstudio, Bildagentur Zoonar GmbH. 16–17 – Tsvetelina

Library of Congress Cataloging-in-Publication Data is available at www.loc.gov or upon request from the publisher.

ISBN: 979-8-88509-975-2 (hardcover)
ISBN: 979-8-88822-154-9 (paperback)
ISBN: 979-8-88822-295-9 (ebook)

© 2024 BookLife Publishing
This edition is published by arrangement with BookLife Publishing.

For more information, write to Bearport Publishing, 5357 Penn Avenue South, Minneapolis, MN 55419.

CONTENTS

COUNTRY TO COUNTRY

Which country do you live in?

A country is an area of land marked by **borders**. The people in each country have their own rules and ways of living. They may speak different languages.

Each country around the world has its own interesting things to see and do. Let's take a trip to visit a country and learn more!

Have you ever visited another country?

TODAY'S TRIP IS TO
SOUTH AFRICA!

ASIA

EUROPE

NORTH AMERICA

AFRICA

SOUTH AMERICA

AUSTRALIA

South Africa

South Africa is a country in the **continent** of Africa.

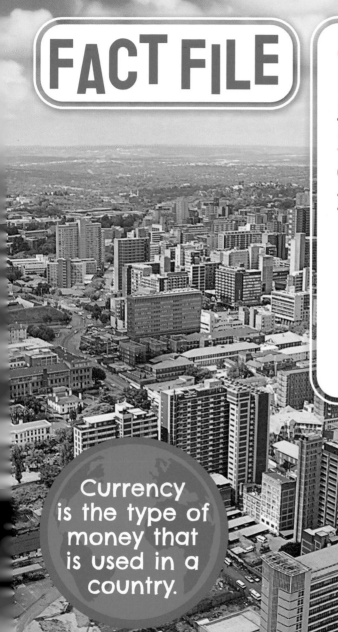

FACT FILE

Capital cities: Pretoria, Bloemfontein, and Cape Town
Main languages: Xhosa, Zulu, and 9 others
Currency: Rand
Flag:

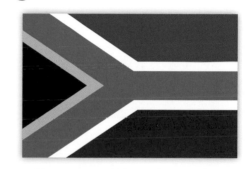

Currency is the type of money that is used in a country.

CAPE TOWN

More than 70 percent of plants on Table Mountain aren't found anywhere else in the world.

We'll start our trip in Cape Town, one of South Africa's capital cities. It is next to a huge mountain with a flat top called Table Mountain. Clouds sometimes cover the top of it.

Not far from Table Mountain, we can find Boulders Beach. Thousands of African penguins live here. They can be seen waddling along the sand.

SPORTS

Sports are very popular in South Africa. The three main sports are soccer, rugby, and cricket. South Africa has one of the best cricket teams in the world.

A sport called jukskei was created in South Africa more than 250 years ago. Jukskei players have to knock a stick over by throwing a peg at it.

KRUGER NATIONAL PARK

Ready to see some **wildlife**? Let's go to Kruger National Park. It has elephants, zebras, giraffes, and more. We might see many different animals drinking from the same waterhole.

Some animals in Kruger National Park, such as black rhinos, are **endangered**. This park is one of the last places black rhinos can be found.

Black rhinoceroses

MOTLATSE CANYON

Motlatse **Canyon** is one of the largest canyons in the world. It has high mountains, many waterfalls, and lots of plant life.

14

In one part of the canyon, water has washed away some of the rock, leaving large holes. These are called Bourke's Luck Potholes. We can look down at them from a bridge.

ZULU PEOPLE

The Zulu people are the largest group of people in South Africa. They are known for their **weaving** and colorful beadwork.

Music and dancing are important in Zulu **culture**. They are a part of many celebrations. Zulu people usually wear **traditional** clothes for their dances.

DRAGON MOUNTAINS

This area is also called Drakensberg.

Next, we'll head to the Dragon Mountains. There, a long wall of **cliffs** spreads out for more than 3 miles (5 km). Some parts of the cliffs are nearly 4,000 feet (1,200 m) tall.

The Dragon Mountains are also home to the second-tallest waterfall in the world. Tugela Falls is more than 3,000 ft (900 m) high.

Tugela Falls

FOOD

Feeling hungry? Let's get some food. Barbecue events called braais are very popular in South Africa. At braais, people visit with one another and eat delicious grilled meat.

Koeksisters are another popular food in South Africa. This sweet dough is twisted before being fried. Then, the crunchy outside is covered in a sticky **syrup**.

BEFORE YOU GO

We can't forget to take a drive on the Garden Route. This road goes along the coast of South Africa. It is a great way to see many beautiful towns, cliffs, and forests.

The Garden Route

We could also go **surfing**. The city of Durban has many beaches with big waves for surfing. Some people even call it Surf City.

What have you learned about South Africa on this trip?

GLOSSARY

borders lines that show where one place ends and another begins

canyon a deep, narrow valley carved out by a river

cliffs high, steep rocks

continent one of the world's seven large land masses

culture the customs and traditions shared by a group of people

endangered in danger of dying out completely

surfing riding waves in the ocean, usually on a surfboard

syrup a sweet, thick liquid

traditional relating to a custom, belief, or way of doing something that has stayed the same for many years

weaving lacing together pieces of material to make something

wildlife wild animals living in their natural setting

INDEX